Dearest Dan, Happy Birthday
All our love
Grandma, Gramps

Bicycle

This Notebook

Belong to:

Daniel

Bicycle Journal

Date: 28.8.2023   Time:

Weather: ☀️ ⛅✓ 🌧️ ☂️ ❄️ ⚡ 🌀

Location Type

Trails

- [x] Roadways
- [ ] Park
- [ ] Forest Trails
- [ ] Mountain Trails
- [x] Other

Route Ratings: 4
Environment Difficulty: 3
Road Condition: 4

Address:
Route: Barnstaple to Okehampton
Route Highlights: Mud bog
GPS:

Bicycle Set Up

Bicycle Type/Notes: Road

Bicycle Accessories: Pentobox, light

Start Time	End Time	Duration	Distance
8.50	17.30	8hr 40m	87 km

Avg Speed	Max Speed	Intensity
18k	45.6 km	kind of hard

Notes

very jumpy ride, on the way to plymouth. I'm excited

Bicycle Journal

Date: 29.8.2023   **Time:**

Weather: ☀️ ⛅ 🌧️ ☂️ ❄️ ⚡ 🌀

Location Type

Trails

- [x] Roadways
- [ ] Park
- [ ] Forest Trails
- [ ] Mountain Trails
- [ ] Other

Route Ratings: 1 2 3 [✓4] 5

Environment Difficulty: 1 2 3 [✓4] 5

Road Condition: 1 2 3 [✓4] 5

Address:

Route: okehampton to plymouth

Route Highlights: rocky road ~~long (not seal)~~

GPS:

Bicycle Set Up

Bicycle Type/Notes: road

Bicycle Accessories: light penbox

Start Time	End Time	Duration	Distance
			60k

Avg Speed	Max Speed	Intensity
	45.6 km	Medium

Notes

Funny ride finished plymouth ride and saw football.

Bicycle Journal

Date: .... Time: [ ]

Weather: ☀️ ⛅ 🌧️ ☂️ ❄️ ⚡ 🌪️

Location Type

....

Roadways ☐ Park ☐ Forest Trails ☐ Mountain Trails ☐ Other ☐

Route Ratings
| 1 | 2 | 3 | 4 | 5 |

Environment Difficulty
| 1 | 2 | 3 | 4 | 5 |

Road Condition
| 1 | 2 | 3 | 4 | 5 |

Address: ....

Route: ....

Route Highlights: .... GPS: ....

Bicycle Set Up

Bicycle Type/Notes

Bicycle Accessories

| Start Time | End Time | Duration | Distance |

| Avg Speed | Max Speed | Intensity |

Notes

....

....

....

Bicycle Journal

Date: ....   Time: [   ]

Weather: ☀️ ⛅ 🌧️ ☂️ ❄️ ⚡ 🌪️

Location Type

....

Roadways ☐   Park ☐   Forest Trails ☐   Mountain Trails ☐   Other ☐

Route Ratings
| 1 | 2 | 3 | 4 | 5 |

Environment Difficulty
| 1 | 2 | 3 | 4 | 5 |

Road Condition
| 1 | 2 | 3 | 4 | 5 |

Address: ....

Route: ....

Route Highlights: .... GPS: ....

Bicycle Set Up

Bicycle Type/Notes

Bicycle Accessories

Start Time	End Time	Duration	Distance

Avg Speed	Max Speed	Intensity

Notes

....

....

....

Bicycle Journal

Date: .... Time: [   ]

Weather: ☀️ ⛅ 🌧️ ☂️ ❄️ ⚡ 🌪️

Location Type

....

Roadways ☐   Park ☐   Forest Trails ☐   Mountain Trails ☐   Other ☐

Route Ratings
1 2 3 4 5

Environment Difficulty
1 2 3 4 5

Road Condition
1 2 3 4 5

Address: ....

Route: ....

Route Highlights: .... GPS: ....

Bicycle Set Up

Bicycle Type/Notes

Bicycle Accessories

Start Time	End Time	Duration	Distance

Avg Speed	Max Speed	Intensity

Notes

....

....

....

Bicycle Journal

Date: .... Time: [   ]

Weather: ☀ ⛅ 🌧 ☂ ❄ ⚡ 🌀

Location Type

....

Roadways ☐ Park ☐ Forest Trails ☐ Mountain Trails ☐ Other ☐

Route Ratings
1 2 3 4 5

Environment Difficulty
1 2 3 4 5

Road Condition
1 2 3 4 5

Address: ....
Route: ....
Route Highlights: .... GPS: ....

Bicycle Set Up

Bicycle Type/Notes

Bicycle Accessories

Start Time	End Time	Duration	Distance

Avg Speed	Max Speed	Intensity

Notes

....
....
....

Bicycle Journal

Date: .... Time:

Weather: ☀ ⛅ 🌧 ☂ ❄ ⚡ 🌀

Location Type

☐ Roadways ☐ Park ☐ Forest Trails ☐ Mountain Trails ☐ Other

Route Ratings
1 2 3 4 5

Environment Difficulty
1 2 3 4 5

Road Condition
1 2 3 4 5

Address: ....
Route: ....
Route Highlights: .... GPS: ....

Bicycle Set Up

Bicycle Type/Notes

Bicycle Accessories

| Start Time | End Time | Duration | Distance |

| Avg Speed | Max Speed | Intensity |

Notes

....
....
....

Bicycle Journal

Date: .... Time:

Weather:

Location Type

....

Roadways ☐   Park ☐   Forest Trails ☐   Mountain Trails ☐   Other ☐

Route Ratings
1 2 3 4 5

Environment Difficulty
1 2 3 4 5

Road Condition
1 2 3 4 5

Address: ....
Route: ....
Route Highlights: .... GPS: ....

Bicycle Set Up

Bicycle Type/Notes

Bicycle Accessories

Start Time	End Time	Duration	Distance

Avg Speed	Max Speed	Intensity

Notes

....
....
....

Bicycle Journal

Date: .... Time:

Weather: ☀️ ⛅ 🌧️ ☂️ ❄️ ⚡ 🌪️

Location Type

☐ Roadways ☐ Park ☐ Forest Trails ☐ Mountain Trails ☐ Other

Route Ratings
1 2 3 4 5

Environment Difficulty
1 2 3 4 5

Road Condition
1 2 3 4 5

Address: ....

Route: ....

Route Highlights: .... GPS: ....

Bicycle Set Up

Bicycle Type/Notes

Bicycle Accessories

Start Time	End Time	Duration	Distance

Avg Speed	Max Speed	Intensity

Notes

....

....

....

Bicycle Journal

Date: .... Time: [　　　　　]

Weather: ☀ ⛅ 🌧 ☂ ❄ ⚡ 🌪

Location Type

....

☐ Roadways ☐ Park ☐ Forest Trails ☐ Mountain Trails ☐ Other

Route Ratings
1 2 3 4 5

Environment Difficulty
1 2 3 4 5

Road Condition
1 2 3 4 5

Address: ....
Route: ....
Route Highlights: .... GPS: ....

Bicycle Set Up

Bicycle Type/Notes

Bicycle Accessories

Start Time	End Time	Duration	Distance

Avg Speed	Max Speed	Intensity

Notes

....
....
....

Bicycle Journal

Date: .... Time: [   ]

Weather: ☀ ⛅ 🌧 ☂ ❄ ⚡ 🌀

Location Type

Roadways ☐   Park ☐   Forest Trails ☐   Mountain Trails ☐   Other ☐

Route Ratings 1 2 3 4 5

Environment Difficulty 1 2 3 4 5

Road Condition 1 2 3 4 5

Address: ....

Route: ....

Route Highlights: .... GPS: ....

Bicycle Set Up

Bicycle Type/Notes

Bicycle Accessories

Start Time	End Time	Duration	Distance

Avg Speed	Max Speed	Intensity

Notes

....

....

....

Bicycle Journal

Date: .... Time: [_____]

Weather: ☀️ ⛅ 🌧️ ☂️ ❄️ ⚡ 🌪️

Location Type

....

Roadways ☐   Park ☐   Forest Trails ☐   Mountain Trails ☐   Other ☐

Route Ratings   **Environment Difficulty**   **Road Condition**
1 2 3 4 5   1 2 3 4 5   1 2 3 4 5

Address: ....

Route: ....

Route Highlights: .... GPS: ....

Bicycle Set Up

Bicycle Type/Notes   **Bicycle Accessories**

Start Time	End Time	Duration	Distance

Avg Speed	Max Speed	Intensity

Notes

....

....

....

Bicycle Journal

Date: .... Time: [   ]

Weather: ☀️ ⛅ 🌧️ ☂️ ❄️ ⚡ 🌪️

Location Type

....

☐ Roadways   ☐ Park   ☐ Forest Trails   ☐ Mountain Trails   ☐ Other

Route Ratings
1 2 3 4 5

Environment Difficulty
1 2 3 4 5

Road Condition
1 2 3 4 5

Address: ....

Route: ....

Route Highlights: .... GPS: ....

Bicycle Set Up

Bicycle Type/Notes

Bicycle Accessories

Start Time	End Time	Duration	Distance

Avg Speed	Max Speed	Intensity

Notes

....

....

....

Bicycle Journal

Date: .... Time: _____

Weather: ☀️ ⛅ 🌧️ ☂️ ❄️ ⚡ 🌀

Location Type

....

Roadways ☐   Park ☐   Forest Trails ☐   Mountain Trails ☐   Other ☐

Route Ratings   **Environment Difficulty**   **Road Condition**
1 2 3 4 5   1 2 3 4 5   1 2 3 4 5

Address: ....

Route: ....

Route Highlights: .... GPS: ....

Bicycle Set Up

Bicycle Type/Notes

Bicycle Accessories

Start Time	End Time	Duration	Distance

Avg Speed	Max Speed	Intensity

Notes

....

....

....

Bicycle Journal

Date: .... Time: [ ]

Weather: ☀ ⛅ 🌧 ☂ ❄ ⚡ 🌪

Location Type

☐ Roadways ☐ Park ☐ Forest Trails ☐ Mountain Trails ☐ Other

Route Ratings
1 2 3 4 5

Environment Difficulty
1 2 3 4 5

Road Condition
1 2 3 4 5

Address: ....

Route: ....

Route Highlights: .... GPS: ....

Bicycle Set Up

Bicycle Type/Notes

Bicycle Accessories

Start Time	End Time	Duration	Distance

Avg Speed	Max Speed	Intensity

Notes

....
....
....

Bicycle Journal

Date: .... Time:

Weather: ☀️ ⛅ 🌧️ ☂️ ❄️ ⚡ 🌪️

Location Type

....

Roadways ☐   Park ☐   Forest Trails ☐   Mountain Trails ☐   Other ☐

Route Ratings
1 2 3 4 5

Environment Difficulty
1 2 3 4 5

Road Condition
1 2 3 4 5

Address: ....
Route: ....
Route Highlights: .... GPS: ....

Bicycle Set Up

Bicycle Type/Notes

Bicycle Accessories

Start Time	End Time	Duration	Distance

Avg Speed	Max Speed	Intensity

Notes

....
....
....

Bicycle Journal

Date: .... Time: [   ]

Weather: ☀️ ⛅ 🌧️ ☂️ ❄️ ⚡ 🌀

Location Type

- ☐ Roadways
- ☐ Park
- ☐ Forest Trails
- ☐ Mountain Trails
- ☐ Other

Route Ratings: 1 2 3 4 5

Environment Difficulty: 1 2 3 4 5

Road Condition: 1 2 3 4 5

Address: ....

Route: ....

Route Highlights: .... GPS: ....

Bicycle Set Up

Bicycle Type/Notes

Bicycle Accessories

Start Time	End Time	Duration	Distance

Avg Speed	Max Speed	Intensity

Notes

....

....

....

Bicycle Journal

Date: .... Time: [_____]

Weather: ☀ ⛅ 🌧 ☂ ❄ ⚡ 🌀

Location Type

Roadways ☐   Park ☐   Forest Trails ☐   Mountain Trails ☐   Other ☐

Route Ratings 1 2 3 4 5

Environment Difficulty 1 2 3 4 5

Road Condition 1 2 3 4 5

Address: ....

Route: ....

Route Highlights: .... GPS: ....

Bicycle Set Up

Bicycle Type/Notes

Bicycle Accessories

Start Time	End Time	Duration	Distance

Avg Speed	Max Speed	Intensity

Notes

....
....
....

Bicycle Journal

Date: .... **Time:** [　　　　]

Weather: ☀️ ⛅ 🌧️ ☂️ ❄️ ⚡ 🌪️

Location Type

Roadways ☐   Park ☐   Forest Trails ☐   Mountain Trails ☐   Other ☐

Route Ratings
1 2 3 4 5

Environment Difficulty
1 2 3 4 5

Road Condition
1 2 3 4 5

Address: ....

Route: ....

Route Highlights: .... GPS: ....

Bicycle Set Up

Bicycle Type/Notes

Bicycle Accessories

| Start Time | End Time | Duration | Distance |

| Avg Speed | Max Speed | Intensity |

Notes

....

....

....

Bicycle Journal

Date: .... Time:

Weather: ☀ ⛅ 🌧 ☂ ❄ ⚡ 🌀

Location Type

....

Roadways ☐   Park ☐   Forest Trails ☐   Mountain Trails ☐   Other ☐

Route Ratings: 1 2 3 4 5
Environment Difficulty: 1 2 3 4 5
Road Condition: 1 2 3 4 5

Address: ....
Route: ....
Route Highlights: .... GPS: ....

Bicycle Set Up

Bicycle Type/Notes

Bicycle Accessories

Start Time	End Time	Duration	Distance

Avg Speed	Max Speed	Intensity

Notes

....
....
....

Bicycle Journal

Date: .... Time:

Weather: ☀ ⛅ 🌧 ☂ ❄ ⚡ 🌀

Location Type

Roadways ☐ Park ☐ Forest Trails ☐ Mountain Trails ☐ Other ☐

Route Ratings
1 2 3 4 5

Environment Difficulty
1 2 3 4 5

Road Condition
1 2 3 4 5

Address: ....
Route: ....
Route Highlights: .... GPS: ....

Bicycle Set Up

Bicycle Type/Notes

Bicycle Accessories

| Start Time | End Time | Duration | Distance |

| Avg Speed | Max Speed | Intensity |

Notes

....
....
....

Bicycle Journal

Date: .... Time: [   ]

Weather: ☀ ⛅ 🌧 ☂ ❄ ⚡ 🌪

Location Type

....

Roadways ☐   Park ☐   Forest Trails ☐   Mountain Trails ☐   Other ☐

Route Ratings   **Environment Difficulty**   **Road Condition**
1 2 3 4 5   1 2 3 4 5   1 2 3 4 5

Address: ....

Route: ....

Route Highlights: .... GPS: ....

Bicycle Set Up

Bicycle Type/Notes

Bicycle Accessories

Start Time	End Time	Duration	Distance

Avg Speed	Max Speed	Intensity

Notes

....

....

....

Bicycle Journal

Date: .... Time: [   ]

Weather: ☀️ ⛅ 🌧️ ☂️ ❄️ ⚡ 🌀

Location Type

☐ Roadways ☐ Park ☐ Forest Trails ☐ Mountain Trails ☐ Other

Route Ratings: 1 2 3 4 5

Environment Difficulty: 1 2 3 4 5

Road Condition: 1 2 3 4 5

Address: ....

Route: ....

Route Highlights: .... GPS: ....

Bicycle Set Up

Bicycle Type/Notes

Bicycle Accessories

Start Time	End Time	Duration	Distance

Avg Speed	Max Speed	Intensity

Notes

....
....
....

Bicycle Journal

Date: .... Time: [ ]

Weather: ☀️ ⛅ 🌧️ ☂️ ❄️ ⚡ 🌪️

Location Type

....

- [ ] Roadways
- [ ] Park
- [ ] Forest Trails
- [ ] Mountain Trails
- [ ] Other

Route Ratings: 1 2 3 4 5

Environment Difficulty: 1 2 3 4 5

Road Condition: 1 2 3 4 5

Address: ....

Route: ....

Route Highlights: .... GPS: ....

Bicycle Set Up

Bicycle Type/Notes

Bicycle Accessories

Start Time	End Time	Duration	Distance

Avg Speed	Max Speed	Intensity

Notes

....

....

....

Bicycle Journal

Date: .... Time: [   ]

Weather: ☀ ⛅ 🌧 ☂ ❄ ⚡ 🌪

Location Type

| Roadways ☐ | Park ☐ | Forest Trails ☐ | Mountain Trails ☐ | Other ☐ |

Route Ratings
1 2 3 4 5

Environment Difficulty
1 2 3 4 5

Road Condition
1 2 3 4 5

Address: ....

Route: ....

Route Highlights: .... GPS: ....

Bicycle Set Up

Bicycle Type/Notes

Bicycle Accessories

| Start Time | End Time | Duration | Distance |

| Avg Speed | Max Speed | Intensity |

Notes

....

....

....

Bicycle Journal

Date: .... Time: [   ]

Weather: ☀️ ⛅ 🌧️ ☂️ ❄️ ⚡ 🌪️

Location Type

....

Roadways ☐   Park ☐   Forest Trails ☐   Mountain Trails ☐   Other ☐

Route Ratings
1 2 3 4 5

Environment Difficulty
1 2 3 4 5

Road Condition
1 2 3 4 5

Address: ....

Route: ....

Route Highlights: .... GPS: ....

Bicycle Set Up

Bicycle Type/Notes

Bicycle Accessories

Start Time	End Time	Duration	Distance

Avg Speed	Max Speed	Intensity

Notes

....

....

....

Bicycle Journal

Date: .... Time: [ ]

Weather: ☀ ⛅ 🌧 ☂ ❄ ⚡ 🌀

Location Type

Roadways ☐   Park ☐   Forest Trails ☐   Mountain Trails ☐   Other ☐

Route Ratings
| 1 | 2 | 3 | 4 | 5 |

Environment Difficulty
| 1 | 2 | 3 | 4 | 5 |

Road Condition
| 1 | 2 | 3 | 4 | 5 |

Address: ....

Route: ....

Route Highlights: .... GPS: ....

Bicycle Set Up

Bicycle Type/Notes

Bicycle Accessories

Start Time	End Time	Duration	Distance

Avg Speed	Max Speed	Intensity

Notes

....

....

....

Bicycle Journal

Date: .... **Time:** [ ]

Weather: ☀️ ⛅ 🌧️ ☂️ ❄️ ⚡ 🌪️

Location Type

....

Roadways	Park	Forest Trails	Mountain Trails	Other
☐	☐	☐	☐	☐

Route Ratings
1 2 3 4 5

Environment Difficulty
1 2 3 4 5

Road Condition
1 2 3 4 5

Address: ....

Route: ....

Route Highlights: .... GPS: ....

Bicycle Set Up

Bicycle Type/Notes

Bicycle Accessories

Start Time	End Time	Duration	Distance

Avg Speed	Max Speed	Intensity

Notes

....

....

....

Bicycle Journal

Date: .... Time:

Weather:

Location Type

Roadways ☐   Park ☐   Forest Trails ☐   Mountain Trails ☐   Other ☐

Route Ratings
1 2 3 4 5

Environment Difficulty
1 2 3 4 5

Road Condition
1 2 3 4 5

Address: ....

Route: ....

Route Highlights: .... GPS: ....

Bicycle Set Up

Bicycle Type/Notes

Bicycle Accessories

| Start Time | End Time | Duration | Distance |

| Avg Speed | Max Speed | Intensity |

Notes

....

....

....

Bicycle Journal

Date: .... Time: []

Weather: ☀ ⛅ 🌧 ☂ ❄ ⚡ 🌪

Location Type

....

- ☐ Roadways
- ☐ Park
- ☐ Forest Trails
- ☐ Mountain Trails
- ☐ Other

Route Ratings 1 2 3 4 5

Environment Difficulty 1 2 3 4 5

Road Condition 1 2 3 4 5

Address: ....

Route: ....

Route Highlights: .... GPS: ....

Bicycle Set Up

Bicycle Type/Notes

Bicycle Accessories

Start Time	End Time	Duration	Distance

Avg Speed	Max Speed	Intensity

Notes

....

....

....

Bicycle Journal

Date: .... Time: [   ]

Weather: ☀️ ⛅ 🌧️ ☂️ ❄️ ⚡ 🌪️

Location Type

Roadways ☐   Park ☐   Forest Trails ☐   Mountain Trails ☐   Other ☐

Route Ratings
☐ ☐ ☐ ☐ ☐
1 2 3 4 5

Environment Difficulty
☐ ☐ ☐ ☐ ☐
1 2 3 4 5

Road Condition
☐ ☐ ☐ ☐ ☐
1 2 3 4 5

Address: ....

Route: ....

Route Highlights: .... GPS: ....

Bicycle Set Up

Bicycle Type/Notes

Bicycle Accessories

Start Time	End Time	Duration	Distance

Avg Speed	Max Speed	Intensity

Notes

....

....

....

Bicycle Journal

Date: .... Time: [   ]

Weather: ☀ ⛅ 🌧 ☂ ❄ ⚡ 🌀

Location Type

....

Roadways ☐   Park ☐   Forest Trails ☐   Mountain Trails ☐   Other ☐

Route Ratings
1 2 3 4 5

Environment Difficulty
1 2 3 4 5

Road Condition
1 2 3 4 5

Address: ....

Route: ....

Route Highlights: .... GPS: ....

Bicycle Set Up

Bicycle Type/Notes

Bicycle Accessories

Start Time	End Time	Duration	Distance

Avg Speed	Max Speed	Intensity

Notes

....

....

....

Bicycle Journal

Date: .... Time: [   ]

Weather: ☀️ ⛅ 🌧️ ☂️ ❄️ ⚡ 🌪️

Location Type

....

Roadways ☐ Park ☐ Forest Trails ☐ Mountain Trails ☐ Other ☐

Route Ratings
1 2 3 4 5

Environment Difficulty
1 2 3 4 5

Road Condition
1 2 3 4 5

Address: ....

Route: ....

Route Highlights: .... GPS: ....

Bicycle Set Up

Bicycle Type/Notes

Bicycle Accessories

Start Time	End Time	Duration	Distance

Avg Speed	Max Speed	Intensity

Notes

....

....

....

Bicycle Journal

Date: .... **Time:** _____

Weather: ☀ ⛅ 🌧 ☂ ❄ ⚡ 🌀

Location Type

....

- ☐ Roadways
- ☐ Park
- ☐ Forest Trails
- ☐ Mountain Trails
- ☐ Other

Route Ratings: 1 2 3 4 5

Environment Difficulty: 1 2 3 4 5

Road Condition: 1 2 3 4 5

Address: ....

Route: ....

Route Highlights: .... GPS: ....

Bicycle Set Up

Bicycle Type/Notes

Bicycle Accessories

Start Time	End Time	Duration	Distance

Avg Speed	Max Speed	Intensity

Notes

....

....

....

Bicycle Journal

Date: .... **Time:** _____

Weather: ☀️ ⛅ 🌧️ ☂️ ❄️ ⚡ 🌪️

Location Type

- [ ] Roadways
- [ ] Park
- [ ] Forest Trails
- [ ] Mountain Trails
- [ ] Other

Route Ratings: 1 2 3 4 5

Environment Difficulty: 1 2 3 4 5

Road Condition: 1 2 3 4 5

Address: ....

Route: ....

Route Highlights: .... GPS: ....

Bicycle Set Up

Bicycle Type/Notes

Bicycle Accessories

Start Time	End Time	Duration	Distance

Avg Speed	Max Speed	Intensity

Notes

....

....

....

Bicycle Journal

Date: .... Time: _____

Weather: ☀️ ⛅ 🌧️ ☂️ ❄️ ⚡ 🌪️

Location Type

....

- ☐ Roadways
- ☐ Park
- ☐ Forest Trails
- ☐ Mountain Trails
- ☐ Other

Route Ratings: 1 2 3 4 5

Environment Difficulty: 1 2 3 4 5

Road Condition: 1 2 3 4 5

Address:..

Route:..

Route Highlights:.. GPS:............

Bicycle Set Up

Bicycle Type/Notes

Bicycle Accessories

Start Time	End Time	Duration	Distance

Avg Speed	Max Speed	Intensity

Notes

....
....
....

Bicycle Journal

Date: .... Time: _____

Weather: ☀️ ⛅ 🌧️ ☂️ ❄️ ⚡ 🌪️

Location Type

☐ Roadways   ☐ Park   ☐ Forest Trails   ☐ Mountain Trails   ☐ Other

Route Ratings
| 1 | 2 | 3 | 4 | 5 |

Environment Difficulty
| 1 | 2 | 3 | 4 | 5 |

Road Condition
| 1 | 2 | 3 | 4 | 5 |

Address: ....

Route: ....

Route Highlights: .... GPS: ....

Bicycle Set Up

Bicycle Type/Notes

Bicycle Accessories

Start Time	End Time	Duration	Distance

Avg Speed	Max Speed	Intensity

Notes

....

....

....

Bicycle Journal

Date: ....   Time: _____

Weather: ☀️ ⛅ 🌧️ ☂️ ❄️ ⚡ 🌀

Location Type

....

Roadways ☐   Park ☐   Forest Trails ☐   Mountain Trails ☐   Other ☐

Route Ratings
| 1 | 2 | 3 | 4 | 5 |

Environment Difficulty
| 1 | 2 | 3 | 4 | 5 |

Road Condition
| 1 | 2 | 3 | 4 | 5 |

Address: ....

Route: ....

Route Highlights: ....   GPS: ....

Bicycle Set Up

Bicycle Type/Notes

Bicycle Accessories

| Start Time | End Time | Duration | Distance |

| Avg Speed | Max Speed | Intensity |

Notes

....

....

....

Bicycle Journal

Date: .... Time: _____

Weather: ☀️ ⛅ 🌧️ ☂️ ❄️ ⚡ 🌪️

Location Type

....

Roadways ☐   Park ☐   Forest Trails ☐   Mountain Trails ☐   Other ☐

Route Ratings   **Environment Difficulty**   **Road Condition**
1 2 3 4 5   1 2 3 4 5   1 2 3 4 5

Address: ....

Route: ....

Route Highlights: .... GPS: ....

Bicycle Set Up

Bicycle Type/Notes

Bicycle Accessories

Start Time	End Time	Duration	Distance

Avg Speed	Max Speed	Intensity

Notes

....

....

....

Bicycle Journal

Date: .... Time: [ ]

Weather: ☀ ⛅ 🌧 ☂ ❄ ⚡ 🌀

Location Type

Roadways ☐   Park ☐   Forest Trails ☐   Mountain Trails ☐   Other ☐

Route Ratings
1 2 3 4 5

Environment Difficulty
1 2 3 4 5

Road Condition
1 2 3 4 5

Address: ....
Route: ....
Route Highlights: .... GPS: ....

Bicycle Set Up

Bicycle Type/Notes

Bicycle Accessories

Start Time	End Time	Duration	Distance

Avg Speed	Max Speed	Intensity

Notes

....
....
....

Bicycle Journal

Date: .... Time:

Weather:

Location Type

Roadways ☐ Park ☐ Forest Trails ☐ Mountain Trails ☐ Other ☐

Route Ratings
1 2 3 4 5

Environment Difficulty
1 2 3 4 5

Road Condition
1 2 3 4 5

Address: ....

Route: ....

Route Highlights: .... GPS: ....

Bicycle Set Up

Bicycle Type/Notes

Bicycle Accessories

| Start Time | End Time | Duration | Distance |

| Avg Speed | Max Speed | Intensity |

Notes

....

....

....

Bicycle Journal

Date: .... Time: [ ]

Weather: ☀️ ⛅ 🌧️ ☂️ ❄️ ⚡ 🌀

Location Type

....

Roadways ☐ Park ☐ Forest Trails ☐ Mountain Trails ☐ Other ☐

Route Ratings
1 2 3 4 5

Environment Difficulty
1 2 3 4 5

Road Condition
1 2 3 4 5

Address: ....
Route: ....
Route Highlights: .... GPS: ....

Bicycle Set Up

Bicycle Type/Notes

Bicycle Accessories

Start Time	End Time	Duration	Distance

Avg Speed	Max Speed	Intensity

Notes

....
....
....

Bicycle Journal

Date: .... Time: _____

Weather: ☀ ⛅ 🌧 ☂ ❄ ⚡ 🌀

Location Type

....

Roadways ☐   Park ☐   Forest Trails ☐   Mountain Trails ☐   Other ☐

Route Ratings
| 1 | 2 | 3 | 4 | 5 |

Environment Difficulty
| 1 | 2 | 3 | 4 | 5 |

Road Condition
| 1 | 2 | 3 | 4 | 5 |

Address:..

Route:..

Route Highlights:... GPS:...........................

Bicycle Set Up

Bicycle Type/Notes

Bicycle Accessories

| Start Time | End Time | Duration | Distance |

| Avg Speed | Max Speed | Intensity |

Notes

....

....

....

Bicycle Journal

Date: .... **Time:** _____

Weather: ☀️ ⛅ 🌧️ ☂️ ❄️ ⚡ 🌪️

Location Type

....

Roadways ☐   Park ☐   Forest Trails ☐   Mountain Trails ☐   Other ☐

Route Ratings
| | | | | |
|—|—|—|—|—|
1 2 3 4 5

Environment Difficulty
| | | | | |
|—|—|—|—|—|
1 2 3 4 5

Road Condition
| | | | | |
|—|—|—|—|—|
1 2 3 4 5

Address: ....

Route: ....

Route Highlights: .... GPS: ....

Bicycle Set Up

Bicycle Type/Notes

Bicycle Accessories

Start Time	End Time	Duration	Distance

Avg Speed	Max Speed	Intensity

Notes

....

....

....

Bicycle Journal

Date: .... **Time:** ☐

Weather: ☀️ ⛅ 🌧️ ☂️ ❄️ ⚡ 🌀

Location Type

Roadways ☐   Park ☐   Forest Trails ☐   Mountain Trails ☐   Other ☐

Route Ratings
1 2 3 4 5

Environment Difficulty
1 2 3 4 5

Road Condition
1 2 3 4 5

Address: ....

Route: ....

Route Highlights: .... GPS: ....

Bicycle Set Up

Bicycle Type/Notes

Bicycle Accessories

Start Time	End Time	Duration	Distance

Avg Speed	Max Speed	Intensity

Notes

....

....

....

Bicycle Journal

Date: .... Time: [ ]

Weather: ☀ ⛅ 🌧 ☂ ❄ ⚡ 🌪

Location Type

Roadways ☐ Park ☐ Forest Trails ☐ Mountain Trails ☐ Other ☐

Route Ratings
1 2 3 4 5

Environment Difficulty
1 2 3 4 5

Road Condition
1 2 3 4 5

Address: ....

Route: ....

Route Highlights: .... GPS: ....

Bicycle Set Up

Bicycle Type/Notes

Bicycle Accessories

| Start Time | End Time | Duration | Distance |

| Avg Speed | Max Speed | Intensity |

Notes

....

....

....

Bicycle Journal

Date: .... Time: _____

Weather: ☀️ ⛅ 🌧️ ☂️ ❄️ ⚡ 🌪️

Location Type

....

Roadways ☐   Park ☐   Forest Trails ☐   Mountain Trails ☐   Other ☐

Route Ratings
| 1 | 2 | 3 | 4 | 5 |

Environment Difficulty
| 1 | 2 | 3 | 4 | 5 |

Road Condition
| 1 | 2 | 3 | 4 | 5 |

Address: ....

Route: ....

Route Highlights: .... GPS: ....

Bicycle Set Up

Bicycle Type/Notes

Bicycle Accessories

Start Time	End Time	Duration	Distance

Avg Speed	Max Speed	Intensity

Notes

....
....
....

Bicycle Journal

Date: .... Time: [   ]

Weather: ☀️ ⛅ 🌧️ ☂️ ❄️ ⚡ 🌪️

Location Type

Roadways ☐   Park ☐   Forest Trails ☐   Mountain Trails ☐   Other ☐

Route Ratings
1 2 3 4 5

Environment Difficulty
1 2 3 4 5

Road Condition
1 2 3 4 5

Address: ....

Route: ....

Route Highlights: .... GPS: ....

Bicycle Set Up

Bicycle Type/Notes

Bicycle Accessories

Start Time	End Time	Duration	Distance

Avg Speed	Max Speed	Intensity

Notes

....

....

....

Bicycle Journal

Date: .... **Time:**

Weather: ☀️ ⛅ 🌧️ ☂️ ❄️ ⚡ 🌀

Location Type

....

Roadways ☐   Park ☐   Forest Trails ☐   Mountain Trails ☐   Other ☐

Route Ratings
| 1 | 2 | 3 | 4 | 5 |

Environment Difficulty
| 1 | 2 | 3 | 4 | 5 |

Road Condition
| 1 | 2 | 3 | 4 | 5 |

Address: ....

Route: ....

Route Highlights: .... GPS: ....

Bicycle Set Up

Bicycle Type/Notes

Bicycle Accessories

Start Time	End Time	Duration	Distance

Avg Speed	Max Speed	Intensity

Notes

....

....

....

Bicycle Journal

Date: .... Time: _____

Weather: ☀️ ⛅ 🌧️ ☂️ ❄️ ⚡ 🌀

Location Type

Roadways ☐   Park ☐   Forest Trails ☐   Mountain Trails ☐   Other ☐

Route Ratings
1 2 3 4 5

Environment Difficulty
1 2 3 4 5

Road Condition
1 2 3 4 5

Address: ....

Route: ....

Route Highlights: .... GPS: ....

Bicycle Set Up

Bicycle Type/Notes

Bicycle Accessories

Start Time	End Time	Duration	Distance

Avg Speed	Max Speed	Intensity

Notes

....
....
....

Bicycle Journal

Date: .... Time: [ ]

Weather: ☀ ⛅ 🌧 ☂ ❄ ⚡ 🌀

Location Type

....

Roadways ☐   Park ☐   Forest Trails ☐   Mountain Trails ☐   Other ☐

Route Ratings
| 1 | 2 | 3 | 4 | 5 |

Environment Difficulty
| 1 | 2 | 3 | 4 | 5 |

Road Condition
| 1 | 2 | 3 | 4 | 5 |

Address: ....

Route: ....

Route Highlights: .... GPS: ....

Bicycle Set Up

Bicycle Type/Notes

Bicycle Accessories

| Start Time | End Time | Duration | Distance |

| Avg Speed | Max Speed | Intensity |

Notes

....
....
....

Bicycle Journal

Date: .... Time: [   ]

Weather: ☀️ ⛅ 🌧️ ☂️ ❄️ ⚡ 🌀

Location Type

....

Roadways ☐   Park ☐   Forest Trails ☐   Mountain Trails ☐   Other ☐

Route Ratings
1 2 3 4 5

Environment Difficulty
1 2 3 4 5

Road Condition
1 2 3 4 5

Address: ....

Route: ....

Route Highlights: .... GPS: ....

Bicycle Set Up

Bicycle Type/Notes

Bicycle Accessories

Start Time	End Time	Duration	Distance

Avg Speed	Max Speed	Intensity

Notes

....

....

....

Bicycle Journal

Date: .... **Time:** ☐

Weather: ☀️ ⛅ 🌧️ ☂️ ❄️ ⚡ 🌪️

Location Type

☐ Roadways ☐ Park ☐ Forest Trails ☐ Mountain Trails ☐ Other

Route Ratings: 1 2 3 4 5

Environment Difficulty: 1 2 3 4 5

Road Condition: 1 2 3 4 5

Address: ....

Route: ....

Route Highlights: .... GPS: ....

Bicycle Set Up

Bicycle Type/Notes

Bicycle Accessories

Start Time	End Time	Duration	Distance

Avg Speed	Max Speed	Intensity

Notes

....

....

....

Bicycle Journal

Date: .... Time: [_____]

Weather: ☀️ ⛅ 🌧️ ☂️ ❄️ ⚡ 🌀

Location Type

- ☐ Roadways
- ☐ Park
- ☐ Forest Trails
- ☐ Mountain Trails
- ☐ Other

Route Ratings
1	2	3	4	5

Environment Difficulty
1	2	3	4	5

Road Condition
1	2	3	4	5

Address: ....

Route: ....

Route Highlights: .... GPS: ....

Bicycle Set Up

Bicycle Type/Notes

Bicycle Accessories

Start Time	End Time	Duration	Distance

Avg Speed	Max Speed	Intensity

Notes

....

....

....

Bicycle Journal

Date: .... **Time:** _____

Weather: ☀️ ⛅ 🌧️ ☂️ ❄️ ⚡ 🌪️

Location Type

☐ Roadways ☐ Park ☐ Forest Trails ☐ Mountain Trails ☐ Other

Route Ratings
| 1 | 2 | 3 | 4 | 5 |

Environment Difficulty
| 1 | 2 | 3 | 4 | 5 |

Road Condition
| 1 | 2 | 3 | 4 | 5 |

Address: ....

Route: ....

Route Highlights: .... GPS: ....

Bicycle Set Up

Bicycle Type/Notes

Bicycle Accessories

| Start Time | End Time | Duration | Distance |

| Avg Speed | Max Speed | Intensity |

Notes

....

....

....

Bicycle Journal

Date: ....   Time: [   ]

Weather: ☀️ ⛅ 🌧️ ☂️ ❄️ ⚡ 🌪️

Location Type

Roadways ☐   Park ☐   Forest Trails ☐   Mountain Trails ☐   Other ☐

Route Ratings
1 2 3 4 5

Environment Difficulty
1 2 3 4 5

Road Condition
1 2 3 4 5

Address: ....

Route: ....

Route Highlights: ....   GPS: ....

Bicycle Set Up

Bicycle Type/Notes

Bicycle Accessories

Start Time	End Time	Duration	Distance

Avg Speed	Max Speed	Intensity

Notes

....

....

....

Bicycle Journal

Date: .... **Time:**

Weather: ☀️ ⛅ 🌧️ ☂️ ❄️ ⚡ 🌪️

Location Type

- [ ] Roadways
- [ ] Park
- [ ] Forest Trails
- [ ] Mountain Trails
- [ ] Other

Route Ratings 1 2 3 4 5

Environment Difficulty 1 2 3 4 5

Road Condition 1 2 3 4 5

Address: ....

Route: ....

Route Highlights: .... GPS: ....

Bicycle Set Up

Bicycle Type/Notes

Bicycle Accessories

Start Time	End Time	Duration	Distance

Avg Speed	Max Speed	Intensity

Notes

....

....

....

Bicycle Journal

Date: .... Time: [ ]

Weather: ☀️ ⛅ 🌧️ ☂️ ❄️ ⚡ 🌀

Location Type

....

- [ ] Roadways
- [ ] Park
- [ ] Forest Trails
- [ ] Mountain Trails
- [ ] Other

Route Ratings: 1 2 3 4 5

Environment Difficulty: 1 2 3 4 5

Road Condition: 1 2 3 4 5

Address: ....
Route: ....
Route Highlights: .... GPS: ....

Bicycle Set Up

Bicycle Type/Notes

Bicycle Accessories

Start Time	End Time	Duration	Distance

Avg Speed	Max Speed	Intensity

Notes

....
....
....

Bicycle Journal

Date: .... Time: _____

Weather: ☀️ ⛅ 🌧️ ☂️ ❄️ ⚡ 🌪️

Location Type

....

☐ Roadways ☐ Park ☐ Forest Trails ☐ Mountain Trails ☐ Other

Route Ratings
| 1 | 2 | 3 | 4 | 5 |

Environment Difficulty
| 1 | 2 | 3 | 4 | 5 |

Road Condition
| 1 | 2 | 3 | 4 | 5 |

Address: ....

Route: ....

Route Highlights: .... GPS: ....

Bicycle Set Up

Bicycle Type/Notes

Bicycle Accessories

| Start Time | End Time | Duration | Distance |

| Avg Speed | Max Speed | Intensity |

Notes

....

....

....

Bicycle Journal

Date: .... Time: [   ]

Weather: ☀ ⛅ 🌧 ☂ ❄ ⚡ 🌪

Location Type

....

Roadways ☐   Park ☐   Forest Trails ☐   Mountain Trails ☐   Other ☐

Route Ratings
1 2 3 4 5

Environment Difficulty
1 2 3 4 5

Road Condition
1 2 3 4 5

Address: ....
Route: ....
Route Highlights: .... GPS: ....

Bicycle Set Up

Bicycle Type/Notes

Bicycle Accessories

Start Time	End Time	Duration	Distance

Avg Speed	Max Speed	Intensity

Notes

....
....
....

Bicycle Journal

Date: .... **Time:** _____

Weather: ☀️ ⛅ 🌧️ ☂️ ❄️ ⚡ 🌪️

Location Type

☐ Roadways ☐ Park ☐ Forest Trails ☐ Mountain Trails ☐ Other

Route Ratings
| 1 | 2 | 3 | 4 | 5 |

Environment Difficulty
| 1 | 2 | 3 | 4 | 5 |

Road Condition
| 1 | 2 | 3 | 4 | 5 |

Address: ....

Route: ....

Route Highlights: .... GPS: ....

Bicycle Set Up

Bicycle Type/Notes

Bicycle Accessories

Start Time	End Time	Duration	Distance

Avg Speed	Max Speed	Intensity

Notes

....

....

....

Bicycle Journal

Date: .... **Time:**

Weather: ☀️ ⛅ 🌧️ ☂️ ❄️ ⚡ 🌪️

Location Type

....

| Roadways ☐ | Park ☐ | Forest Trails ☐ | Mountain Trails ☐ | Other ☐ |

Route Ratings
1 2 3 4 5

Environment Difficulty
1 2 3 4 5

Road Condition
1 2 3 4 5

Address: ....

Route: ....

Route Highlights: .... GPS: ....

Bicycle Set Up

Bicycle Type/Notes

Bicycle Accessories

| Start Time | End Time | Duration | Distance |

| Avg Speed | Max Speed | Intensity |

Notes

....
....
....

Bicycle Journal

Date: .... Time: [   ]

Weather: ☀️ ⛅ 🌧️ ☂️ ❄️ ⚡ 🌪️

Location Type

Roadways ☐   Park ☐   Forest Trails ☐   Mountain Trails ☐   Other ☐

Route Ratings
| 1 | 2 | 3 | 4 | 5 |

Environment Difficulty
| 1 | 2 | 3 | 4 | 5 |

Road Condition
| 1 | 2 | 3 | 4 | 5 |

Address: ....

Route: ....

Route Highlights: .... GPS: ....

Bicycle Set Up

Bicycle Type/Notes

Bicycle Accessories

| Start Time | End Time | Duration | Distance |

| Avg Speed | Max Speed | Intensity |

Notes

....

....

....

Bicycle Journal

Date: .... Time: [ ]

Weather: ☀️ ⛅ 🌧️ ☂️ ❄️ ⚡ 🌪️

Location Type

....

Roadways ☐   Park ☐   Forest Trails ☐   Mountain Trails ☐   Other ☐

Route Ratings
1 2 3 4 5

Environment Difficulty
1 2 3 4 5

Road Condition
1 2 3 4 5

Address: ....

Route: ....

Route Highlights: .... GPS: ....

Bicycle Set Up

Bicycle Type/Notes

Bicycle Accessories

Start Time	End Time	Duration	Distance

Avg Speed	Max Speed	Intensity

Notes

....

....

....

Bicycle Journal

Date: .... Time: [　　　　　　]

Weather: ☀️ ⛅ 🌧️ ☂️ ❄️ ⚡ 🌪️

Location Type

....

- [ ] Roadways
- [ ] Park
- [ ] Forest Trails
- [ ] Mountain Trails
- [ ] Other

Route Ratings: 1 2 3 4 5

Environment Difficulty: 1 2 3 4 5

Road Condition: 1 2 3 4 5

Address: ....

Route: ....

Route Highlights: .... GPS: ....

Bicycle Set Up

Bicycle Type/Notes

Bicycle Accessories

Start Time	End Time	Duration	Distance

Avg Speed	Max Speed	Intensity

Notes

....

....

....

Bicycle Journal

Date: ....   Time: _____

Weather: ☀️ ⛅ 🌧️ ☂️ ❄️ ⚡ 🌪️

Location Type

Roadways ☐   Park ☐   Forest Trails ☐   Mountain Trails ☐   Other ☐

Route Ratings
1 2 3 4 5

Environment Difficulty
1 2 3 4 5

Road Condition
1 2 3 4 5

Address: ....

Route: ....

Route Highlights: .... GPS: ....

Bicycle Set Up

Bicycle Type/Notes

Bicycle Accessories

| Start Time | End Time | Duration | Distance |

| Avg Speed | Max Speed | Intensity |

Notes

....
....
....

Bicycle Journal

Date: .... **Time:**

Weather: ☀️ ⛅ 🌧️ ☂️ ❄️ ⚡ 🌪️

Location Type

Roadways ☐   Park ☐   Forest Trails ☐   Mountain Trails ☐   Other ☐

Route Ratings
1 2 3 4 5

Environment Difficulty
1 2 3 4 5

Road Condition
1 2 3 4 5

Address: ....

Route: ....

Route Highlights: ....   GPS: ....

Bicycle Set Up

Bicycle Type/Notes

Bicycle Accessories

Start Time	End Time	Duration	Distance

Avg Speed	Max Speed	Intensity

Notes

....

....

....

Bicycle Journal

Date: .... Time: [   ]

Weather: ☀️ ⛅ 🌧️ ☂️ ❄️ ⚡ 🌪️

Location Type

- ☐ Roadways
- ☐ Park
- ☐ Forest Trails
- ☐ Mountain Trails
- ☐ Other

Route Ratings: 1 2 3 4 5

Environment Difficulty: 1 2 3 4 5

Road Condition: 1 2 3 4 5

Address: ....

Route: ....

Route Highlights: .... GPS: ....

Bicycle Set Up

Bicycle Type/Notes

Bicycle Accessories

Start Time	End Time	Duration	Distance

Avg Speed	Max Speed	Intensity

Notes

....

....

....

Bicycle Journal

Date: .... Time: [   ]

Weather: ☀️ ⛅ 🌧️ ☂️ ❄️ ⚡ 🌪️

Location Type

- ☐ Roadways
- ☐ Park
- ☐ Forest Trails
- ☐ Mountain Trails
- ☐ Other

Route Ratings: 1 2 3 4 5

Environment Difficulty: 1 2 3 4 5

Road Condition: 1 2 3 4 5

Address: ....

Route: ....

Route Highlights: .... GPS: ....

Bicycle Set Up

Bicycle Type/Notes

Bicycle Accessories

Start Time	End Time	Duration	Distance

Avg Speed	Max Speed	Intensity

Notes

....

....

....

Bicycle Journal

Date: .... Time:

Weather: ☀ ⛅ 🌧 ☂ ❄ ⚡ 🌪

Location Type

....

Roadways ☐   Park ☐   Forest Trails ☐   Mountain Trails ☐   Other ☐

Route Ratings
1 2 3 4 5

Environment Difficulty
1 2 3 4 5

Road Condition
1 2 3 4 5

Address:..

Route:..

Route Highlights:... GPS:..............................

Bicycle Set Up

Bicycle Type/Notes

Bicycle Accessories

| Start Time | End Time | Duration | Distance |

| Avg Speed | Max Speed | Intensity |

Notes

....

....

....

Bicycle Journal

Date: .... Time:

Weather: ☀️ ⛅ 🌧️ ☂️ ❄️ ⚡ 🌪️

Location Type

Roadways ☐   Park ☐   Forest Trails ☐   Mountain Trails ☐   Other ☐

Route Ratings
1 2 3 4 5

Environment Difficulty
1 2 3 4 5

Road Condition
1 2 3 4 5

Address: ....

Route: ....

Route Highlights: .... GPS: ....

Bicycle Set Up

Bicycle Type/Notes

Bicycle Accessories

| Start Time | End Time | Duration | Distance |

| Avg Speed | Max Speed | Intensity |

Notes

....
....
....

Bicycle Journal

Date: .... **Time:** [   ]

Weather: ☀️ ⛅ 🌧️ ☂️ ❄️ ⚡ 🌪️

Location Type

....

- ☐ Roadways
- ☐ Park
- ☐ Forest Trails
- ☐ Mountain Trails
- ☐ Other

Route Ratings: 1 2 3 4 5

Environment Difficulty: 1 2 3 4 5

Road Condition: 1 2 3 4 5

Address:..

Route:..

Route Highlights:... GPS:...

Bicycle Set Up

Bicycle Type/Notes

Bicycle Accessories

Start Time	End Time	Duration	Distance

Avg Speed	Max Speed	Intensity

Notes

....

....

....

Bicycle Journal

Date: .... Time:

weather: ☀ ⛅ 🌧 ☂ ❄ ⚡ 🌀

Location Type

☐ Roadways ☐ Park ☐ Forest Trails ☐ Mountain Trails ☐ Other

Route Ratings
1 2 3 4 5

Environment Difficulty
1 2 3 4 5

Road Condition
1 2 3 4 5

Address: ....

Route: ....

Route Highlights: .... GPS: ....

Bicycle Set Up

Bicycle Type/Notes

Bicycle Accessories

| Start Time | End Time | Duration | Distance |

| Avg Speed | Max Speed | Intensity |

Notes

....

....

....

Bicycle Journal

Date: .... Time:

Weather:

Location Type

....

Roadways ☐   Park ☐   Forest Trails ☐   Mountain Trails ☐   Other ☐

Route Ratings
1 2 3 4 5

Environment Difficulty
1 2 3 4 5

Road Condition
1 2 3 4 5

Address:...

Route:..

Route Highlights:..................................... GPS:..............

Bicycle Set Up

Bicycle Type/Notes

Bicycle Accessories

| Start Time | End Time | Duration | Distance |

| Avg Speed | Max Speed | Intensity |

Notes

....

....

....

Bicycle Journal

Date: .... Time:

Weather: ☀ ⛅ 🌧 ☂ ❄ ⚡ 🌀

Location Type

....

- ☐ Roadways
- ☐ Park
- ☐ Forest Trails
- ☐ Mountain Trails
- ☐ Other

Route Ratings: 1 2 3 4 5

Environment Difficulty: 1 2 3 4 5

Road Condition: 1 2 3 4 5

Address: ....

Route: ....

Route Highlights: .... GPS: ....

Bicycle Set Up

Bicycle Type/Notes

Bicycle Accessories

Start Time	End Time	Duration	Distance

Avg Speed	Max Speed	Intensity

Notes

....

....

....

Bicycle Journal

Date: .... Time: [   ]

Weather: ☀ ⛅ 🌧 ☂ ❄ ⚡ 🌀

Location Type

Roadways ☐   Park ☐   Forest Trails ☐   Mountain Trails ☐   Other ☐

Route Ratings
1 2 3 4 5

Environment Difficulty
1 2 3 4 5

Road Condition
1 2 3 4 5

Address: ....

Route: ....

Route Highlights: .... GPS: ....

Bicycle Set Up

Bicycle Type/Notes

Bicycle Accessories

Start Time	End Time	Duration	Distance

Avg Speed	Max Speed	Intensity

Notes

....

....

....

Bicycle Journal

Date: .... Time: _____

Weather: ☀️ ⛅ 🌧️ ☂️ ❄️ ⚡ 🌪️

Location Type

- [ ] Roadways
- [ ] Park
- [ ] Forest Trails
- [ ] Mountain Trails
- [ ] Other

Route Ratings
1 2 3 4 5

Environment Difficulty
1 2 3 4 5

Road Condition
1 2 3 4 5

Address: ....

Route: ....

Route Highlights: .... GPS: ....

Bicycle Set Up

Bicycle Type/Notes

Bicycle Accessories

Start Time	End Time	Duration	Distance

Avg Speed	Max Speed	Intensity

Notes

....
....
....

Bicycle Journal

Date: .... Time: _____

Weather: ☀️ ⛅ 🌧️ ☂️ ❄️ ⚡ 🌀

Location Type

....

☐ Roadways ☐ Park ☐ Forest Trails ☐ Mountain Trails ☐ Other

Route Ratings
1 2 3 4 5

Environment Difficulty
1 2 3 4 5

Road Condition
1 2 3 4 5

Address: ....

Route: ....

Route Highlights: .... GPS: ....

Bicycle Set Up

Bicycle Type/Notes

Bicycle Accessories

Start Time	End Time	Duration	Distance

Avg Speed	Max Speed	Intensity

Notes

....
....
....

Bicycle Journal

Date: .... Time: [ ]

Weather: ☀️ ⛅ 🌧️ ☂️ ❄️ ⚡ 🌪️

Location Type

....

☐ Roadways ☐ Park ☐ Forest Trails ☐ Mountain Trails ☐ Other

Route Ratings
1 2 3 4 5

Environment Difficulty
1 2 3 4 5

Road Condition
1 2 3 4 5

Address: ....

Route: ....

Route Highlights: .... GPS: ....

Bicycle Set Up

Bicycle Type/Notes

Bicycle Accessories

Start Time	End Time	Duration	Distance

Avg Speed	Max Speed	Intensity

Notes

....

....

....

Bicycle Journal

Date: .... Time: _____

Weather: ☀️ ⛅ 🌧️ ☂️ ❄️ ⚡ 🌪️

Location Type

- [ ] Roadways
- [ ] Park
- [ ] Forest Trails
- [ ] Mountain Trails
- [ ] Other

Route Ratings: 1 2 3 4 5

Environment Difficulty: 1 2 3 4 5

Road Condition: 1 2 3 4 5

Address: ....

Route: ....

Route Highlights: .... GPS: ....

Bicycle Set Up

Bicycle Type/Notes

Bicycle Accessories

Start Time	End Time	Duration	Distance

Avg Speed	Max Speed	Intensity

Notes

....

....

....

Bicycle Journal

Date: .... Time: [ ]

Weather: ☀️ ⛅ 🌧️ ☂️ ❄️ ⚡ 🌪️

Location Type

Roadways ☐ Park ☐ Forest Trails ☐ Mountain Trails ☐ Other ☐

Route Ratings
1 2 3 4 5

Environment Difficulty
1 2 3 4 5

Road Condition
1 2 3 4 5

Address: ....

Route: ....

Route Highlights: .... GPS: ....

Bicycle Set Up

Bicycle Type/Notes

Bicycle Accessories

Start Time	End Time	Duration	Distance

Avg Speed	Max Speed	Intensity

Notes

....
....
....

Bicycle Journal

Date: .... **Time:** ☐

Weather: ☀️ ⛅ 🌧️ ☂️ ❄️ ⚡ 🌀

Location Type

....

☐ Roadways   ☐ Park   ☐ Forest Trails   ☐ Mountain Trails   ☐ Other

Route Ratings 1 2 3 4 5

Environment Difficulty 1 2 3 4 5

Road Condition 1 2 3 4 5

Address: ....

Route: ....

Route Highlights: .... GPS: ....

Bicycle Set Up

Bicycle Type/Notes

Bicycle Accessories

Start Time	End Time	Duration	Distance

Avg Speed	Max Speed	Intensity

Notes

....

....

....

Bicycle Journal

Date: .... Time: _____

Weather: ☀️ ⛅ 🌧️ ☂️ ❄️ ⚡ 🌪️

Location Type

- [ ] Roadways
- [ ] Park
- [ ] Forest Trails
- [ ] Mountain Trails
- [ ] Other

Route Ratings
1 2 3 4 5

Environment Difficulty
1 2 3 4 5

Road Condition
1 2 3 4 5

Address: ....

Route: ....

Route Highlights: .... GPS: ....

Bicycle Set Up

Bicycle Type/Notes

Bicycle Accessories

Start Time	End Time	Duration	Distance

Avg Speed	Max Speed	Intensity

Notes

....

....

....

Bicycle Journal

Date: .... Time: _____

Weather: ☀ ⛅ 🌧 ☂ ❄ ⚡ 🌀

Location Type

....

Roadways ☐   Park ☐   Forest Trails ☐   Mountain Trails ☐   Other ☐

Route Ratings 1 2 3 4 5

Environment Difficulty 1 2 3 4 5

Road Condition 1 2 3 4 5

Address: ....

Route: ....

Route Highlights: .... GPS: ....

Bicycle Set Up

Bicycle Type/Notes

Bicycle Accessories

Start Time	End Time	Duration	Distance

Avg Speed	Max Speed	Intensity

Notes

....

....

....

Bicycle Journal

Date: .... Time:

Weather: ☀ ⛅ 🌧 ☂ ❄ ⚡ 🌪

Location Type

....

- ☐ Roadways
- ☐ Park
- ☐ Forest Trails
- ☐ Mountain Trails
- ☐ Other

Route Ratings: 1 2 3 4 5

Environment Difficulty: 1 2 3 4 5

Road Condition: 1 2 3 4 5

Address: ....

Route: ....

Route Highlights: .... GPS: ....

Bicycle Set Up

Bicycle Type/Notes

Bicycle Accessories

Start Time	End Time	Duration	Distance

Avg Speed	Max Speed	Intensity

Notes

....

....

....

Bicycle Journal

Date: ....   Time: [   ]

Weather: ☀️ ⛅ 🌧️ ☂️ ❄️ ⚡ 🌀

Location Type

....

Roadways ☐   Park ☐   Forest Trails ☐   Mountain Trails ☐   Other ☐

Route Ratings   **Environment Difficulty**   **Road Condition**
1 2 3 4 5   1 2 3 4 5   1 2 3 4 5

Address: ....

Route: ....

Route Highlights: .... GPS: ....

Bicycle Set Up

Bicycle Type/Notes

Bicycle Accessories

Start Time	End Time	Duration	Distance

Avg Speed	Max Speed	Intensity

Notes

....

....

....

Bicycle Journal

Date: .... Time: [ ]

Weather: ☀️ ⛅ 🌧️ ☂️ ❄️ ⚡ 🌪️

Location Type

Roadways ☐   Park ☐   Forest Trails ☐   Mountain Trails ☐   Other ☐

Route Ratings
1 2 3 4 5

Environment Difficulty
1 2 3 4 5

Road Condition
1 2 3 4 5

Address:..

Route:...

Route Highlights:............................... GPS:...................

Bicycle Set Up

Bicycle Type/Notes

Bicycle Accessories

Start Time	End Time	Duration	Distance

Avg Speed	Max Speed	Intensity

Notes

....
....
....

Bicycle Journal

Date: .... Time: [   ]

Weather: ☀️ ⛅ 🌧️ ☂️ ❄️ ⚡ 🌪️

Location Type

- ☐ Roadways
- ☐ Park
- ☐ Forest Trails
- ☐ Mountain Trails
- ☐ Other

Route Ratings: 1 2 3 4 5

Environment Difficulty: 1 2 3 4 5

Road Condition: 1 2 3 4 5

Address: ....

Route: ....

Route Highlights: .... GPS: ....

Bicycle Set Up

Bicycle Type/Notes

Bicycle Accessories

Start Time	End Time	Duration	Distance

Avg Speed	Max Speed	Intensity

Notes

....

....

....

Bicycle Journal

Date: .... Time: ☐

Weather: ☀️ ⛅ 🌧️ ☂️ ❄️ ⚡ 🌪️

Location Type

Roadways ☐   Park ☐   Forest Trails ☐   Mountain Trails ☐   Other ☐

Route Ratings
1 2 3 4 5

Environment Difficulty
1 2 3 4 5

Road Condition
1 2 3 4 5

Address: ....

Route: ....

Route Highlights: .... GPS: ....

Bicycle Set Up

Bicycle Type/Notes

Bicycle Accessories

| Start Time | End Time | Duration | Distance |

| Avg Speed | Max Speed | Intensity |

Notes

....
....
....

Bicycle Journal

Date: .... Time: [   ]

Weather: ☀ ⛅ 🌧 ☂ ❄ ⚡ 🌀

Location Type

....

- ☐ Roadways
- ☐ Park
- ☐ Forest Trails
- ☐ Mountain Trails
- ☐ Other

Route Ratings 1 2 3 4 5

Environment Difficulty 1 2 3 4 5

Road Condition 1 2 3 4 5

Address:..

Route:..

Route Highlights:.. GPS:..............................

Bicycle Set Up

Bicycle Type/Notes

Bicycle Accessories

Start Time	End Time	Duration	Distance

Avg Speed	Max Speed	Intensity

Notes

....

....

....

Bicycle Journal

Date: .... Time:

Weather: ☀️ ⛅ 🌧️ ☂️ ❄️ ⚡ 🌪️

Location Type

☐ Roadways ☐ Park ☐ Forest Trails ☐ Mountain Trails ☐ Other

Route Ratings
1 2 3 4 5

Environment Difficulty
1 2 3 4 5

Road Condition
1 2 3 4 5

Address: ....

Route: ....

Route Highlights: .... GPS: ....

Bicycle Set Up

Bicycle Type/Notes

Bicycle Accessories

| Start Time | End Time | Duration | Distance |

| Avg Speed | Max Speed | Intensity |

Notes

....

....

....

Bicycle Journal

Date: .... Time:

Weather:

Location Type

- [ ] Roadways
- [ ] Park
- [ ] Forest Trails
- [ ] Mountain Trails
- [ ] Other

Route Ratings: 1 2 3 4 5

Environment Difficulty: 1 2 3 4 5

Road Condition: 1 2 3 4 5

Address: ....

Route: ....

Route Highlights: .... GPS: ....

Bicycle Set Up

Bicycle Type/Notes

Bicycle Accessories

Start Time	End Time	Duration	Distance

Avg Speed	Max Speed	Intensity

Notes

....

....

....

Bicycle Journal

Date: .... Time: [   ]

Weather: ☀️ ⛅ 🌧️ ☂️ ❄️ ⚡ 🌀

Location Type

Roadways ☐   Park ☐   Forest Trails ☐   Mountain Trails ☐   Other ☐

Route Ratings
1 2 3 4 5

Environment Difficulty
1 2 3 4 5

Road Condition
1 2 3 4 5

Address: ....

Route: ....

Route Highlights: .... GPS: ....

Bicycle Set Up

Bicycle Type/Notes

Bicycle Accessories

| Start Time | End Time | Duration | Distance |

| Avg Speed | Max Speed | Intensity |

Notes

....

....

....

Bicycle Journal

Date: .... Time: [   ]

Weather: ☀ ⛅ 🌧 ☂ ❄ ⚡ 🌀

Location Type

....

- ☐ Roadways
- ☐ Park
- ☐ Forest Trails
- ☐ Mountain Trails
- ☐ Other

Route Ratings
1 2 3 4 5

Environment Difficulty
1 2 3 4 5

Road Condition
1 2 3 4 5

Address: ....

Route: ....

Route Highlights: .... GPS: ....

Bicycle Set Up

Bicycle Type/Notes

Bicycle Accessories

Start Time	End Time	Duration	Distance

Avg Speed	Max Speed	Intensity

Notes

....

....

....

Bicycle Journal

Date: .... Time: [ ]

Weather: ☀ ⛅ 🌧 ☂ ❄ ⚡ 🌪

Location Type

....

Roadways ☐   Park ☐   Forest Trails ☐   Mountain Trails ☐   Other ☐

Route Ratings
| 1 | 2 | 3 | 4 | 5 |

Environment Difficulty
| 1 | 2 | 3 | 4 | 5 |

Road Condition
| 1 | 2 | 3 | 4 | 5 |

Address:..

Route:...

Route Highlights:.. GPS:..

Bicycle Set Up

Bicycle Type/Notes

Bicycle Accessories

Start Time	End Time	Duration	Distance

Avg Speed	Max Speed	Intensity

Notes

....
....
....

Bicycle Journal

Date: .... Time: [ ]

Weather: ☀️ ⛅ 🌧️ ☂️ ❄️ ⚡ 🌪️

Location Type

Roadways ☐ Park ☐ Forest Trails ☐ Mountain Trails ☐ Other ☐

Route Ratings
1 2 3 4 5

Environment Difficulty
1 2 3 4 5

Road Condition
1 2 3 4 5

Address: ....

Route: ....

Route Highlights: .... GPS: ....

Bicycle Set Up

Bicycle Type/Notes

Bicycle Accessories

Start Time	End Time	Duration	Distance

Avg Speed	Max Speed	Intensity

Notes

....
....
....

Bicycle Journal

Date: .... Time:

Weather:

Location Type

Roadways ☐   Park ☐   Forest Trails ☐   Mountain Trails ☐   Other ☐

Route Ratings
1 2 3 4 5

Environment Difficulty
1 2 3 4 5

Road Condition
1 2 3 4 5

Address: ....

Route: ....

Route Highlights: .... GPS: ....

Bicycle Set Up

Bicycle Type/Notes

Bicycle Accessories

| Start Time | End Time | Duration | Distance |

| Avg Speed | Max Speed | Intensity |

Notes

....

....

....

Bicycle Journal

Date: .... Time: [   ]

Weather: ☀️ ⛅ 🌧️ ☂️ ❄️ ⚡ 🌀

Location Type

....

☐ Roadways ☐ Park ☐ Forest Trails ☐ Mountain Trails ☐ Other

Route Ratings
1 2 3 4 5

Environment Difficulty
1 2 3 4 5

Road Condition
1 2 3 4 5

Address: ....

Route: ....

Route Highlights: .... GPS: ....

Bicycle Set Up

Bicycle Type/Notes

Bicycle Accessories

| Start Time | End Time | Duration | Distance |

| Avg Speed | Max Speed | Intensity |

Notes

....

....

....

Bicycle Journal

Date: .... Time: [ ]

Weather: ☀️ ⛅ 🌧️ ☂️ ❄️ ⚡ 🌪️

Location Type

....

Roadways ☐   Park ☐   Forest Trails ☐   Mountain Trails ☐   Other ☐

Route Ratings
| 1 | 2 | 3 | 4 | 5 |

Environment Difficulty
| 1 | 2 | 3 | 4 | 5 |

Road Condition
| 1 | 2 | 3 | 4 | 5 |

Address: ....

Route: ....

Route Highlights: .... GPS: ....

Bicycle Set Up

Bicycle Type/Notes

Bicycle Accessories

| Start Time | End Time | Duration | Distance |

| Avg Speed | Max Speed | Intensity |

Notes

....

....

....

Bicycle Journal

Date: .... Time: [   ]

Weather: ☀️ ⛅ 🌧️ ☂️ ❄️ ⚡ 🌀

Location Type

....

Roadways ☐   Park ☐   Forest Trails ☐   Mountain Trails ☐   Other ☐

Route Ratings
1 2 3 4 5

Environment Difficulty
1 2 3 4 5

Road Condition
1 2 3 4 5

Address: ....

Route: ....

Route Highlights: .... GPS: ....

Bicycle Set Up

Bicycle Type/Notes

Bicycle Accessories

Start Time	End Time	Duration	Distance

Avg Speed	Max Speed	Intensity

Notes

....
....
....

Bicycle Journal

Date: .... Time: [   ]

Weather: ☀️ ⛅ 🌧️ ☂️ ❄️ ⚡ 🌪️

Location Type

....

Roadways ☐   Park ☐   Forest Trails ☐   Mountain Trails ☐   Other ☐

Route Ratings
| 1 | 2 | 3 | 4 | 5 |

Environment Difficulty
| 1 | 2 | 3 | 4 | 5 |

Road Condition
| 1 | 2 | 3 | 4 | 5 |

Address: ....

Route: ....

Route Highlights: .... GPS: ....

Bicycle Set Up

Bicycle Type/Notes

Bicycle Accessories

Start Time	End Time	Duration	Distance

Avg Speed	Max Speed	Intensity

Notes

....

....

....

Bicycle Journal

Date: .... Time: [   ]

Weather: ☀ ⛅ 🌧 ☂ ❄ ⚡ 🌪

Location Type

Roadways ☐ Park ☐ Forest Trails ☐ Mountain Trails ☐ Other ☐

Route Ratings: 1 2 3 4 5

Environment Difficulty: 1 2 3 4 5

Road Condition: 1 2 3 4 5

Address: ....

Route: ....

Route Highlights: .... GPS: ....

Bicycle Set Up

Bicycle Type/Notes

Bicycle Accessories

Start Time	End Time	Duration	Distance

Avg Speed	Max Speed	Intensity

Notes

....

....

....

Bicycle Journal

Date: .... Time:

Weather: ☀️ ⛅ 🌧️ ☂️ ❄️ ⚡ 🌪️

Location Type

....

- [ ] Roadways
- [ ] Park
- [ ] Forest Trails
- [ ] Mountain Trails
- [ ] Other

Route Ratings: 1 2 3 4 5

Environment Difficulty: 1 2 3 4 5

Road Condition: 1 2 3 4 5

Address: ....

Route: ....

Route Highlights: .... GPS: ....

Bicycle Set Up

Bicycle Type/Notes

Bicycle Accessories

Start Time	End Time	Duration	Distance

Avg Speed	Max Speed	Intensity

Notes

....
....
....

Bicycle Journal

Date: .... Time: [ ]

Weather: ☀ ⛅ 🌧 ☂ ❄ ⚡ 🌀

Location Type

☐ Roadways ☐ Park ☐ Forest Trails ☐ Mountain Trails ☐ Other

Route Ratings
1 2 3 4 5

Environment Difficulty
1 2 3 4 5

Road Condition
1 2 3 4 5

Address: ....

Route: ....

Route Highlights: .... GPS: ....

Bicycle Set Up

Bicycle Type/Notes

Bicycle Accessories

Start Time	End Time	Duration	Distance

Avg Speed	Max Speed	Intensity

Notes

....
....
....

Bicycle Journal

Date: .... Time: [ ]

Weather: ☀️ ⛅ 🌧️ ☂️ ❄️ ⚡ 🌀

Location Type

....

- ☐ Roadways
- ☐ Park
- ☐ Forest Trails
- ☐ Mountain Trails
- ☐ Other

Route Ratings
1 2 3 4 5

Environment Difficulty
1 2 3 4 5

Road Condition
1 2 3 4 5

Address: ....

Route: ....

Route Highlights: .... GPS: ....

Bicycle Set Up

Bicycle Type/Notes

Bicycle Accessories

Start Time	End Time	Duration	Distance

Avg Speed	Max Speed	Intensity

Notes

....

....

....

Bicycle Journal

Date: .... Time: [   ]

Weather: ☀ ⛅ 🌧 ☂ ❄ ⚡ 🌪

Location Type

....

- ☐ Roadways
- ☐ Park
- ☐ Forest Trails
- ☐ Mountain Trails
- ☐ Other

Route Ratings: 1 2 3 4 5

Environment Difficulty: 1 2 3 4 5

Road Condition: 1 2 3 4 5

Address: ....

Route: ....

Route Highlights: .... GPS: ....

Bicycle Set Up

Bicycle Type/Notes

Bicycle Accessories

Start Time	End Time	Duration	Distance

Avg Speed	Max Speed	Intensity

Notes

....

....

....

Bicycle Journal

Date: ....   Time:

Weather:

Location Type

Roadways ☐   Park ☐   Forest Trails ☐   Mountain Trails ☐   Other ☐

Route Ratings
| 1 | 2 | 3 | 4 | 5 |

Environment Difficulty
| 1 | 2 | 3 | 4 | 5 |

Road Condition
| 1 | 2 | 3 | 4 | 5 |

Address: ....

Route: ....

Route Highlights: .... GPS: ....

Bicycle Set Up

Bicycle Type/Notes

Bicycle Accessories

| Start Time | End Time | Duration | Distance |

| Avg Speed | Max Speed | Intensity |

Notes

....

....

....

Bicycle Journal

Date: .... Time: [   ]

Weather: ☀️ ⛅ 🌧️ ☂️ ❄️ ⚡ 🌪️

Location Type

- ☐ Roadways
- ☐ Park
- ☐ Forest Trails
- ☐ Mountain Trails
- ☐ Other

Route Ratings: 1 2 3 4 5

Environment Difficulty: 1 2 3 4 5

Road Condition: 1 2 3 4 5

Address: ....

Route: ....

Route Highlights: .... GPS: ....

Bicycle Set Up

Bicycle Type/Notes

Bicycle Accessories

Start Time	End Time	Duration	Distance

Avg Speed	Max Speed	Intensity

Notes

....
....
....

Bicycle Journal

Date: .... Time: [ ]

Weather: ☀️ ⛅ 🌧️ ☂️ ❄️ ⚡ 🌪️

Location Type

Roadways ☐ Park ☐ Forest Trails ☐ Mountain Trails ☐ Other ☐

Route Ratings: 1 2 3 4 5

Environment Difficulty: 1 2 3 4 5

Road Condition: 1 2 3 4 5

Address: ....

Route: ....

Route Highlights: .... GPS: ....

Bicycle Set Up

Bicycle Type/Notes

Bicycle Accessories

Start Time	End Time	Duration	Distance

Avg Speed	Max Speed	Intensity

Notes

....
....
....

Bicycle Journal

Date: .... Time: _____

Weather: ☀️ ⛅ 🌧️ ☂️ ❄️ ⚡ 🌪️

Location Type

....

- ☐ Roadways
- ☐ Park
- ☐ Forest Trails
- ☐ Mountain Trails
- ☐ Other

Route Ratings: 1 2 3 4 5

Environment Difficulty: 1 2 3 4 5

Road Condition: 1 2 3 4 5

Address: ....

Route: ....

Route Highlights: .... GPS: ....

Bicycle Set Up

Bicycle Type/Notes

Bicycle Accessories

Start Time	End Time	Duration	Distance

Avg Speed	Max Speed	Intensity

Notes

....

....

....

Bicycle Journal

Date: .... Time: [ ]

Weather: ☀️ ⛅ 🌧️ ☂️ ❄️ ⚡ 🌪️

Location Type

....

Roadways ☐   Park ☐   Forest Trails ☐   Mountain Trails ☐   Other ☐

Route Ratings
| 1 | 2 | 3 | 4 | 5 |

Environment Difficulty
| 1 | 2 | 3 | 4 | 5 |

Road Condition
| 1 | 2 | 3 | 4 | 5 |

Address: ....

Route: ....

Route Highlights: .... GPS: ....

Bicycle Set Up

Bicycle Type/Notes

Bicycle Accessories

| Start Time | End Time | Duration | Distance |

| Avg Speed | Max Speed | Intensity |

Notes

....

....

....

Bicycle Journal

Date: .... Time: [   ]

Weather: ☀️ ⛅ 🌧️ ☂️ ❄️ ⚡ 🌪️

Location Type

- [ ] Roadways
- [ ] Park
- [ ] Forest Trails
- [ ] Mountain Trails
- [ ] Other

Route Ratings: 1 2 3 4 5

Environment Difficulty: 1 2 3 4 5

Road Condition: 1 2 3 4 5

Address: ....

Route: ....

Route Highlights: .... GPS: ....

Bicycle Set Up

Bicycle Type/Notes

Bicycle Accessories

Start Time	End Time	Duration	Distance

Avg Speed	Max Speed	Intensity

Notes

....

....

....

Bicycle Journal

Date: ....   Time:

Weather:

Location Type

Roadways ☐   Park ☐   Forest Trails ☐   Mountain Trails ☐   Other ☐

Route Ratings
1 2 3 4 5

Environment Difficulty
1 2 3 4 5

Road Condition
1 2 3 4 5

Address: ....

Route: ....

Route Highlights: ....   GPS: ....

Bicycle Set Up

Bicycle Type/Notes

Bicycle Accessories

| Start Time | End Time | Duration | Distance |

| Avg Speed | Max Speed | Intensity |

Notes

....
....
....

Bicycle Journal

Date: .... Time: [ ]

Weather: ☀ ⛅ 🌧 ☂ ❄ ⚡ 🌪

Location Type

....

- [ ] Roadways
- [ ] Park
- [ ] Forest Trails
- [ ] Mountain Trails
- [ ] Other

Route Ratings 1 2 3 4 5

Environment Difficulty 1 2 3 4 5

Road Condition 1 2 3 4 5

Address: ....
Route: ....
Route Highlights: .... GPS: ....

Bicycle Set Up

Bicycle Type/Notes

Bicycle Accessories

Start Time	End Time	Duration	Distance

Avg Speed	Max Speed	Intensity

Notes

....
....
....

Bicycle Journal

Date: .... Time:

Weather:

Location Type

....

- [ ] Roadways
- [ ] Park
- [ ] Forest Trails
- [ ] Mountain Trails
- [ ] Other

Route Ratings
1 2 3 4 5

Environment Difficulty
1 2 3 4 5

Road Condition
1 2 3 4 5

Address: ....

Route: ....

Route Highlights: .... GPS: ....

Bicycle Set Up

Bicycle Type/Notes

Bicycle Accessories

Start Time	End Time	Duration	Distance

Avg Speed	Max Speed	Intensity

Notes

....

....

....

Bicycle Journal

Date: .... Time: [   ]

Weather: ☀ ⛅ 🌧 ☂ ❄ ⚡ 🌀

Location Type

....

☐ Roadways ☐ Park ☐ Forest Trails ☐ Mountain Trails ☐ Other

Route Ratings
1 2 3 4 5

Environment Difficulty
1 2 3 4 5

Road Condition
1 2 3 4 5

Address: ....

Route: ....

Route Highlights: .... GPS: ....

Bicycle Set Up

Bicycle Type/Notes

Bicycle Accessories

| Start Time | End Time | Duration | Distance |

| Avg Speed | Max Speed | Intensity |

Notes

....
....
....

Bicycle Journal

Date: .... Time: []

Weather: ☀️ ⛅ 🌧️ ☂️ ❄️ ⚡ 🌀

Location Type

- ☐ Roadways
- ☐ Park
- ☐ Forest Trails
- ☐ Mountain Trails
- ☐ Other

Route Ratings: 1 2 3 4 5

Environment Difficulty: 1 2 3 4 5

Road Condition: 1 2 3 4 5

Address: ....

Route: ....

Route Highlights: .... GPS: ....

Bicycle Set Up

Bicycle Type/Notes

Bicycle Accessories

Start Time	End Time	Duration	Distance

Avg Speed	Max Speed	Intensity

Notes

....

....

....

Bicycle Journal

Date: .... Time: _____

Weather: ☀ ⛅ 🌧 ☂ ❄ ⚡ 🌪

Location Type

☐ Roadways ☐ Park ☐ Forest Trails ☐ Mountain Trails ☐ Other

Route Ratings
1 2 3 4 5

Environment Difficulty
1 2 3 4 5

Road Condition
1 2 3 4 5

Address: ....

Route: ....

Route Highlights: .... GPS: ....

Bicycle Set Up

Bicycle Type/Notes

Bicycle Accessories

Start Time	End Time	Duration	Distance

Avg Speed	Max Speed	Intensity

Notes

....

....

....

Bicycle Journal

Date: .... Time: [ ]

Weather: ☀️ ⛅ 🌧️ ☂️ ❄️ ⚡ 🌪️

Location Type

Roadways ☐   Park ☐   Forest Trails ☐   Mountain Trails ☐   Other ☐

Route Ratings
1 2 3 4 5

Environment Difficulty
1 2 3 4 5

Road Condition
1 2 3 4 5

Address: ....

Route: ....

Route Highlights: .... GPS: ....

Bicycle Set Up

Bicycle Type/Notes

Bicycle Accessories

Start Time	End Time	Duration	Distance

Avg Speed	Max Speed	Intensity

Notes

....

....

....

Bicycle Journal

Date: .... Time: [ ]

Weather: ☀️ ⛅ 🌧️ ☂️ ❄️ ⚡ 🌪️

Location Type

....

Roadways ☐   Park ☐   Forest Trails ☐   Mountain Trails ☐   Other ☐

Route Ratings   **Environment Difficulty**   **Road Condition**
1 2 3 4 5   1 2 3 4 5   1 2 3 4 5

Address: ....

Route: ....

Route Highlights: ....   GPS: ....

Bicycle Set Up

Bicycle Type/Notes

Bicycle Accessories

| Start Time | End Time | Duration | Distance |

| Avg Speed | Max Speed | Intensity |

Notes

....

....

....

Bicycle Journal

Date: .... Time: [   ]

Weather: ☀️ ⛅ 🌧️ ☂️ ❄️ ⚡ 🌪️

Location Type

Roadways ☐ Park ☐ Forest Trails ☐ Mountain Trails ☐ Other ☐

Route Ratings
1 2 3 4 5

Environment Difficulty
1 2 3 4 5

Road Condition
1 2 3 4 5

Address: ....

Route: ....

Route Highlights: .... GPS: ....

Bicycle Set Up

Bicycle Type/Notes

Bicycle Accessories

| Start Time | End Time | Duration | Distance |

| Avg Speed | Max Speed | Intensity |

Notes

....

....

....

Bicycle Journal

Date: .... **Time:** _____

Weather: ☀️ ⛅ 🌧️ ☂️ ❄️ ⚡ 🌪️

Location Type

....

- [ ] Roadways
- [ ] Park
- [ ] Forest Trails
- [ ] Mountain Trails
- [ ] Other

Route Ratings: 1 2 3 4 5

Environment Difficulty: 1 2 3 4 5

Road Condition: 1 2 3 4 5

Address:..

Route:..

Route Highlights:.. GPS:....................................

Bicycle Set Up

Bicycle Type/Notes

Bicycle Accessories

Start Time	End Time	Duration	Distance

Avg Speed	Max Speed	Intensity

Notes

....

....

....

Printed in Great Britain
by Amazon